Forest Maiden

Adaptations from

'Kaviyarasu' Na. Kamarasan's Poetries

in english

Sanna Ratnavel

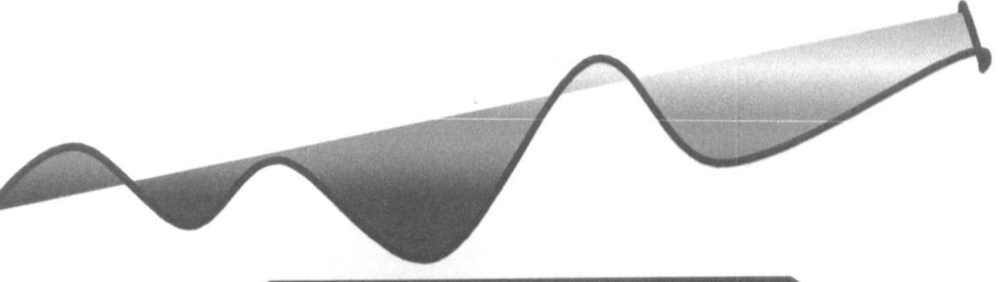

Kaviyarasu Na.Kamarasan

The success of new verses in poetry owes much to the pioneering contributions of poets **like Na.Kamarasan**, whose initial works in this genre are truly remarkable. - Highlighted by **Kamil Václav Zvelebil** is a Czech scholar in Indian literature and linguistics, notably Tamil, Sanskrit, and Tamil sibling linguistics literature and philology.

Contents

*****

Foreword

Translating from classical languages to English presents formidable challenges, demanding not only linguistic skill but also an acute understanding of the poet's tricky intentions and cultural shades. My husband, Kaviyarasu.Na.Kamarasan, a luminary poet reminiscent of Wordsworth, Kamban, Bharathi and Tagore, gathered extensive acclaim for his profound verses and lyrical contributions to Tamil cinema.

My younger brother, Dr.Sanna Ratnavel, fortunate to share the same cultural background, undertook the monumental task of translating Kaviyarasu.Na.Kamarasan's works into English.

 Despite his demanding schedule, Dr.Sanna Ratnavel approached the endeavor with unwavering dedication, resulting in a meticulously crafted collection that has reaped praise from both literary scholars and Eminent poet Na.Kamarasan's inner circle. I extend my profound gratitude to Dr.Sanna Ratnavel for realizing Na.Ka's aspiration to introduce his works to a broader audience.

May Dr.Sanna Ratnavel find continued success in his future endeavors. As readers explore into these English renditions, may they discover not only the beauty of the poetry but also the rich embroidery of cultural connections it offers.

I extend my heartfelt wishes to the translating author, publishers, readers, and all who supported and encouraged this ambitious journey

Yours Faithfully

Logamani Kamarasan

(W/O Kaviyarasu Na.Kamarasan)

25.04.2024

Preface

The Forest Maiden – Adapted from the work of a Tamil 'Poet Laureate' Na.Kamarasan. In this adaptation, an English rendition of the poem was crafted by Dr.Sanna.Ratnavel, a devoted admirer of the epic poet Kaviyarasu Na.Kamarasan.

During the process of translating the poem, it was presented to esteemed scholars and writers in English, who provided several valuable suggestions for improvements.

The majority of these suggestions were accepted and integrated while staying true to the original poet's intentions. To further refine the content, many eminent scholars assistance was also sought on multiple occasions.

After thorough reviews and revisions, the final version of the poem was concluded with the thought-provoking quote,

"Is there any knowledge available in the world, which is not questioned by reasonable persons?"

Adapting Eminent Poet NA.KA's works into any other language proves to be quite challenging due to the highly classic nature of both the poet and the language itself.

Ultimately, it is the readers who serve as the eventual referees, interpreting poems and transforming them into tangible pieces of literature.

Thanking you

Sanna Ratnavel

Date: 14.04.2024

Acknowledgments

I express my sincere gratitude to my respected sister, Mrs. Logamani Kamarasan, wife of the eminent poet Na.Kamarasan, for her continual encouragement, and to the friends and family of the eminent poet Na.Ka., for their firm support throughout this endeavor, this, despite being delayed over the years, has finally come to realization.

Additionally, I take this opportunity to thank Dr.R.Dhanasekaran, Chief Editor, New Vanakkam Thamizhnadu providing content for the prologue. Furthermore, I extend my thanks to the publishers for their exceptional digital support, which has facilitated the realization of this book in a timely manner.

Sanna Ratanvel

PROLOGUE

Poetry in traditional languages, especially classical ones like Tamil, adheres to strict grammatical rules and complex structures, parallel to mathematical equations.

It's widely acknowledged in world literature that language is among the oldest forms of expression, with literary traditions spanning millennia.

 His poems serve to elevate the living standards of the working class while also criticizing the hollow celebrations of festivals and their impact on these individuals' living standards.

In this regard, the works of Kaviyarasu Na. Kamarasan have obtained significant attention from common men, eminent scholars, film producers and academics in various universities.

What's particularly striking about his poetry is his solid respect for the working class. Rather than patronizing or disregarding them, he dignifies their existence by prominently featuring them in his verses.

Through his words, he instills a sense of esteem for the deprived even before policies or reforms are enacted. It's a testament to his reverence for both the language and the simplicity of the lives he portrays.

In honoring the poet and his contributions to literature, we also pay honour to the language, Dr.Sanna Ratnavel, so beautifully put forth the classic shades in the English versions of poems.

Dr.R.Dhanasekaran, M.A, M.Phil.D.Litt,

Chief Editor, New Vanakkam Thamizhnadu.

Adaptation from Na.Kamarasan.

In English Sanna Ratnavel

1. The Faces Found in Signatures

Signatures……

Draw the faces

On the paper

As the streets of commemorations!

As the stripes of the sun

After the darkness of tiredness,

The letters spark at the tip

Of a god's term pen

In the distance apartment,

When the light warm-up the sky

The stars line up on the paper,

As the crown of thorns accomplices

Those scattered and shattered

In to smithereens!

This rises with visibility…

When searching for legs

Leaving their fingered imprints!

After scribbling the above,

The pen left with no drop of ink,

When the cap of the pen is removed,

The erosion of small

The scribbling instrument is exposed,

The faces of life immersed in the tiny manual,

Like a hankie in the hands of ages,

The faces were drawn on my paper leaf

From the signatures,

Those vanished and depreciated

And at last,

It ends with nothingness.

The 'nothingness' is a paper of yesterday

 Lying in the dustbin!

When you pick it up with your fingers,

There, a thousand faces are visible

 In the art form of sketches

I realized now

The world is not "Nothingness"

But a Throne!

*****

2. The Kite Man

The Kites are visible summaries

Of vanishing wind..!

The wings of kites are broken

While competes the wings of winds-

These paper kids practice

The wind as turning swings,

It flies away from the origin of departure,

And pursue it over again from another origin

There is no fire,

Thread and burst sound,

But it guises silent colorful fireworks

Kite images born on the paintbrush!

It debuts impromptu Dances at the elevated sky!

Kites show their head in the direction of the sky

And tail to the earth

Imitates snakes while on display..!

Kites squeeze the small clouds

To crown the lightning this lines earth…!

My heart flies far away leaving me

Oh dear Kite man!

Offer me a pair of wings too..!

*****

3. The Stars and Street Lights

In the perfume of mango tree,

The deer leaping in the grove,

The African black forest beetle,

Composing a song in its way of style,

A blackish sickle harvesting

The hook spinning over again and again!

Afresh green scent leaves

Turn into tiny straws,

The chariot of love god,

Not yet reached to bring my better half!

Undermining the joyful smile,

Causes flowers to fall from

Glorious orchard

And turns into dried fallen leaves!

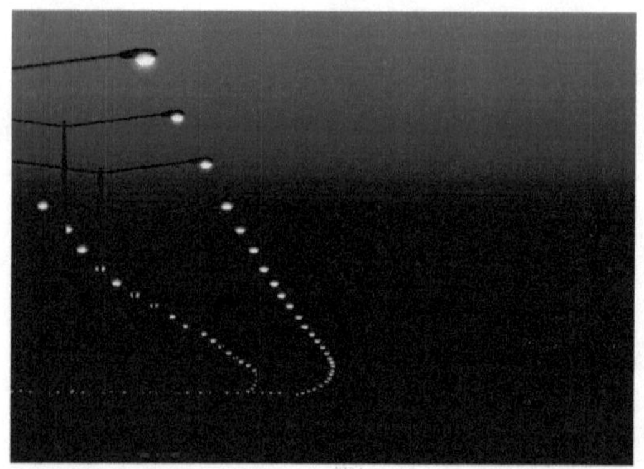

The mind murmurs along

With anklets noise,

Contrary to her young time of life!

Silk cotton tree waits

On the bank of the lake,

It certainly is not a hangman tree,

For the pair of parrots?!

Oh! Better half thrown the stone

In jasmine orchard

If I climb the mountain

Shall you rub me with marigold?!

You drank water

Afterward biting gooseberry,

I am drenched in my tears

As you left me uttering no words?!

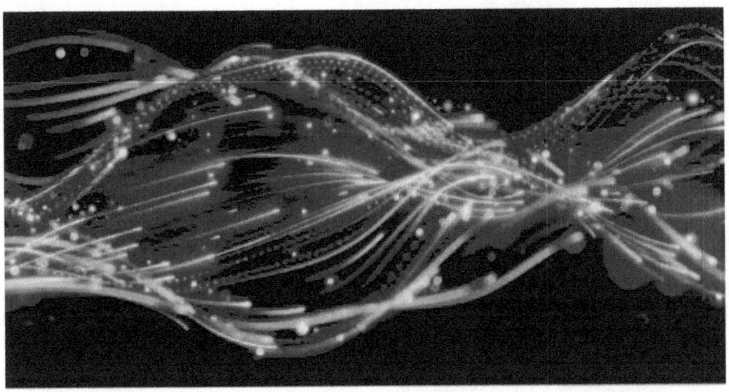

Closing your eyelashes to invoke sleep

And when the dream is in the session,

You touched the sky

On standing 'peak of Himalayas'

Have you touched it?

And thus romanticized with the milky moon?

As my shape slenderized and walking thin

Thus a wound in my heart

Corded golden chariot shall dry

For instance straw in my hands!

My eyes guise like fish

When there is a shower

The sin is steaming on the parabolic

Crescent moon forehead!

A string of pearls just turned into a rope

Hence, the sky stars looks like a street lamp?!

*****

4. Under the feet of this Smile

At the foot of this smile

The time of ocean tide shall blow

Until now, the foam tears of human

Unable to reach the shore

Turns like pearls here…!

A cruel frenzy of violence

Shall turn as coral reef

Silently through frozen blood penance…!

This small rose

While at the stage of budding,

All the thorns shall fall like snow

After blooming the fragrance shall outshine,

Soothing attar perfume….!

The mother of peace shall sleep

On the white rug of this baby's lap,

Adaptation from Na.Kamarasan.   In English Sanna Ratnavel

A toothless smile is the soul

Of a new world without war..!

The skilful art of god Brahma

Trickery arising for the future,

In the unarmed

Small hands of each finger!

The sigh of this bouquet

Sprinkle the poisonous gas...

And the bomb is in the dusk of flame.

During the baby's toddling age

The borders of the world shall vanish

And demonstrate along in one line….!

Harness this child

And let's construct a crib

Then it shall build a graveyard for violence…!

****

5. The Forest Maiden

At the rear of the raised harvesting floor,

In the playful wind of the mango tree,

Clasping a golden beetle in her hands,

A forest maiden sings exuberantly.

It is time to revolve around the globe

With the dream angel's fragrant words

It snoops the dialogue of those blue-eyes

In the form of my heartbeats..!

A thousand flowers hold this jasmine

Her body axis is a tiny mound with flowers,

The maid is built with flowers

as a gorgeous courtyard

Oh..! The devotee turns as mad..?!

Her playful anger hoisted the flag,

The bunch of her flowery hairs

Blowing in the air,

With her reddish, hypnotizing,

Sensual eyes…

She burnt the love landmass in the sky!

She habitually harvests sweet potato

She desires to rest on the sandal tree

She feeds many sweetest small fruits

This forest maiden strolls around

In habitat streets!

She weaves the basket; she catches the 'quail',

Fetching a classic horn honey for sale

The skilful work paints artistic expression

In the stage of her figure shape!

Forecast the dreams

of prospective pride.

 Sitting in their courtyard,

As a proud forest queen

Drive away the love to the vicinity.

Being a symbol of poor...

She portrays dignity

in iron façade clothing

She touches all eight directions

In her revolving eyes

And blinks her eyelashes!

She shakes her bracelets and giggles frequently,

Her anklets chime and twist,

She laughs.

She moves with grace, like a temple dove,

She adorns the colourful porch above,

In the dream tower, she peers and dreams.

As the flowers invade in her walk…

The spear and sword reside

in her agile movement

Catching the moon by her flash glance

The paradise spread the carpet for her foot

As time crosses the boundary

She rushes to search for her porridge pot!

*****

6. Enjoyers of Bonfire

A blazing nest unfurls at the plinth level,

Like a colossal fiery bird

Spreading its wings!

Thus, a bonfire engulfs the trash,

And slumbers within the ash!

The smoke dances upon the rostrum.

It kindles the bowl of mist,

Thus erects an altar on honey springs,

a sacrificial fire..!

The folks gather around the campfire

Cupping their hands

Like fluid in their armpit,

Assuming meditation positions,

Palms displayed,

Before the palpable glow of the fire!

Careful not to forego the warmth,

They maintain a secure distance,

As the gentle flicker embraces their chins!

The fire reflects in the eyes of the ash cat,

Amidst the radiance of the sun,

As it awakens from the platform of crossfire!

*****

7. The Earth

The masses of ice and snow,

Flowers too,

Spreads vast areas of mountains and rivers,

Demonstrating pure traces of nature…!

As the tip of a man's finger touches the sky,

With the power of science,

Thus it plays with the sun's rays

Then passes through holes in torn ozone layers…!

Nature is the mother of human beings,

Thus, the mountain peak ascends beyond-

Above the poisonous smoke

Spewing through implants…!

Adaptation from Na.Kamarasan.   In English Sanna Ratnavel

Womenfolk gather humming golden beetles,

From the forest grove,

Eyes of fire throw the bombs;

Turning the habitats into barren forest

Here motherhood assumes the divinity!

When weapons transform into hands…

The earth goes through cycles of destruction!

Once hands turn into weapons…

Spring flourishes with flowers!

*****

8. The Song of Emptiness

Sabotage squad with 'King's Chamber Umbrella'

Invades with procession from all four sides,

In the horrendous waves of the poisonous river,

A tributary leads violent boats!

On the other bank of the port

Recites the death chanting

The angel of sorrows demands prey!

Even in the heat of the fire

In the smoke of the exploded bombs

Towers melt down into ashes!

Still, the manifesto of the rule turns into void!

The platforms with colourful lights hold,

A series of 'congratulatory' meetings!

Hitler was the one who spread lies blindfolded

He disappeared like a corpse from a dream!

*****

9. Offshore Sea Inhabitants

When I seek you in my bed,

You exist within my heart.

When I search for you in delight,

You sing in the pulse of my heartbeats!

You track me,

 In both day and night,

And hunt me with shadows!

You appear to swim in my visualization,

I see you in the glittery moon rays!

Your lips graze the fence;

My heart blossoms with flowers!

The desert is my sandy domicile

A snowflake to me is an ocean of milk!

You ripen completely,

And fall onto the soil

You sprout from that seed!

You are the womb of

Those three desirable fruits!

You wander like a gipsy,

And you were my nomad's folk song!

I hear the sound of waves like a sailor,

And lean on you as if you were my shore!

*****

10. The Lone Tree Quilt

In that voice the dumbness finds speeches

A monster in the open forest

Streaming like a large streaked tiger!

Summer storm shaken over again

A distant grove makes its call

When the motions of the storm turn silent

The voice of that quill touches the sky!

The sun wheel turns and fades

In the form of the dark cloudy sky

The sound of birds touches the nest

Peeping to the council of the night!

That is the full moonlight of the rainy season

The colour fades and the smoke settles!

No way to live

Like the eyes of a poor charity..!

The dawn is writing the morning

Eyes bloom on the ground

In the focused vision of one of our eyes!

There is a procession of a thousand full moons!

The sun shines like sandalwood...

Thus speaks…

That there are no more poor people!

****

11. The Circular Canoe

A Circular Coracle

Seem beyond the flow field

And the voyage continues in the wind

At the knock of the perfect midnight

It floats in the shadow

Of the starlight's flaming beam

Moving on the river surface

Imagining the ocean!

Sea fishes clouding like frenzy reef fishes

Like the drops of a storm

Crashing the net!

With a single paddle

Beyond the vacuum of poverty

A boatman's heartthrobs,

In the milky moonlight!

Like the hands of an ocean king

The river waves surge!

The heart of the lover floats in a dream,

And dives into the eyes

Thus coracle touches

The shore when it snows!

There the moon's face is seen

In the river through the waves

The music of tomorrow's dawn shall be added!

*****

12. The Tree

In the age to come

Let us bury the living being

The body shall rise

and shake its head in the future!

The eyes hold the flame of the soul

Leaving the cemetery forest

And stepping on the earth!

For the practice of comfort sleep

That shall look the shadow

Of roadside tree!

In those shadows

Not only the sun

The wood fire

Of death shall lie headlong!

Only the shadow does not burn!

Green dreams fall off

while ripening in old age...

The sky shall become the head

And bear moon fruit and star flowers!

When the "rain sends down roots"...

Who plucked the fruit and flower?

Again bearing flowers,

Brewing and ripening...

At the corner of the endless age of the forest

The tree of that time stands strong!

*****

13. The Clay Soil

The blackish soil,

In the rainy season gets washed

Over again and over again

The water gets muddy!

The black soil burns

The root of sprouts with its thirst

The Clay Soil

When sprouts do not grow

Grown sprouts thus perish

The sunny days

Teach thirst to this clay

Though the clay

Drinks nectar once in a while…

Death never approaches the black soil…!

*****

14. The Human Mother

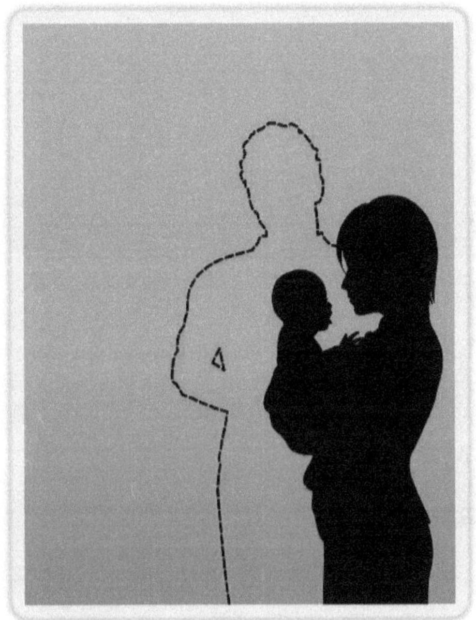

I am the Son of God

The widowed daughter

of the virgin mother

On the bank of the river

I get drenched in the rain

without drinking water

Why did the begging bowl break?

When it does not receive

Breadcrumbs from the church…!

I break the snail nests

In search of food for the saviour...!

The flute that came to announce

Winning and losing

in wrestling was mute..!

Gold dust from a comet

They decorated the broom...!

After I became paralyzed

I created the scriptures...!

Here are the artificial legs

They convert its religion…!

So I crawl on,

Seeking the Kingdom of God..!

My unborn children in my lap….

Have become abandoned seed fruit

In the basket of past times..!

Isn't man higher than religion?

After my husband left me

I became the mother

of an abandoned child..!

Human beliefs are greater than God's

They save this earth..!

Oh... divine prince

I am not a Christian widow...

But a Human mother..!

*****

15. The Poetry of Sage Viyaasan

As he rolled over in bed

After dropping within eight feet trench

What is the wisdom?

Of standing after scorching?

Is it the anger of the time-bound lamp?

In the trick of witchcraft…!

Who is the source?

Come to my ear and say..!

That was the smoke flag that caused the fire

The calculation made by the claimant..!

The potter who makes the pots

Breaks the philosophy- And

Men create history

Thru drifting tireless efforts

Forests too rise..?

Adaptation from Na.Kamarasan.   In English Sanna Ratnavel

How do fruit trees fall?

Plants, turn into lone trees

Tell me what's trendy..?

While crossing the storm over the shore

Pose your head up and stand…!

The temple was built on

Pouring a bunch of pearls at the base

The tower of the temple turns into ashes

On offering ignite the camphor

Are all virtues?

According to the scriptures, a sin?

Even after dint of labour,

Lives end life like a fairy tale

It is a curse,

Thanks to the author of the scripture,

The Sage Viyaasan..!

Is the cemetery the place?

To go in search of a home?

We get Camel's back… - And

Our meditation glows like our poems

On a single-track path...!

*****

16. I am the Sky, I am the Sky Lark

In my silent universe

I observe the glowing full moon,

As I softly close my eyes...!

In the mug of my imaginative milk

I augment the triple divisions of wisdom extract

And swallow the essence of three ages of time,

Thus, I have sworn myself as the Great Poet..!

Who elevates the earth towards the spaces!?

I don't need any nest

When the ears turn out to be nests

I shall sing justice in memecylon heavens!

Clouds shall turn into peaceful huts

There the rainbow forms the crib

The lightening shall turn into a glowing lamp

The eight directions oblige as windows

In the incredible noise of striking clouds

The milk vessel may roll up and down

A dark cat catches the moon

It is imaginable to assume pleasant sleep

Even at the sizzling heat waves of the sun.

*****

Adaptation from Na.Kamarasan.   In English Sanna Ratnavel

17. The Justice for Love

Who has rendered justice, dear Angel?

Again and again, the justice for love gets defeated!

This is a long journey-

I don't have any companions yet!

In the deep darkness,

I feel the heaviest weight on my head!

Your 'Palace' is at the end of this lonely path!

The dreams dissolve in the

'Yesterday and Today's'

They may come tomorrow,

'in the rains of tears'…

A bird flew high with its wings

And fell on this soil with a crucifix on its back

The sins created a grape garden

But the heart donates its blood!

I touch the tides of the perennial river

And it gives me a feeling of touching

The hottest sand in the desert!

The angel bears you in his heart

Now sleeping in the death house!

You tried to wear

The strings of flowers for our wedding

But you brought flowers

For my graveyard!

*****

18. The Old Full Moon

Every family was hoping for the

Acacia fruit is like a reserved pack of food…!

Muddy built stove fire

Has tuned into the celestial sun

The Home lamp has become a white moon

Life has turned for them alien...!

Tubers turn like rice balls

Seed rice is a graceful treat

Water turns into porridge

All of them prevail

In the influence of famine…!

A rose garden merges with saffron

As the red clay floor desiccated...!

In the mango grove

There is a glowing new moon

Thus the old man tries to embed

An old full moon in his mind.

*****

19. They

The burden bearers

Those are well familiar with the plough

They are distant kinfolks

Those are innate natives of this land..!

They recite the story of sword-throwing

Still, they are invisible creatures…!

They perceive the sky

While sleeping in the gunny bags..!

When they examine the sun

Through black clouds in the peak sky,

They suffer injuries

Still, the lightning is absent on their horizon…!

They may not be aware of reading and writing

But they realize that tilling the soil

Though they harvest for the sake of the province

They still starve in poverty…!

They shelter the stomach

And shoulders with ropes

Thus continue the voyage on foot

To fetch the sky…!

*****

20. The Crushed Scrapped Paper

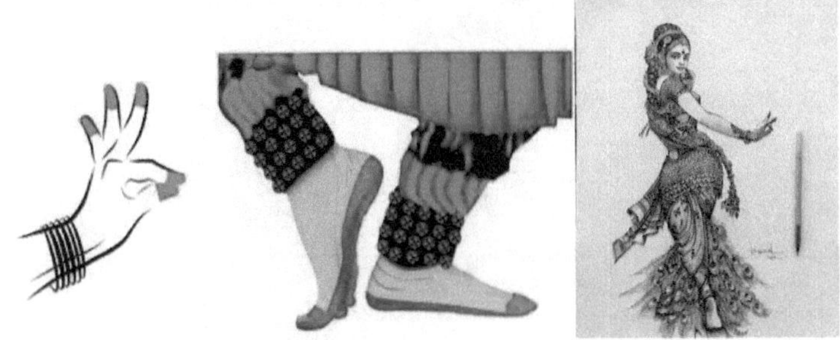

The crushed scrap papers

Her eyes look more enchanted than

Capricorn fish and Musk deer too

She arrogantly travels like a beautiful peak mountain

Thus she creates the great Himalayan

Makes scatters and falls

At her feet into smithereens…!

The beverage of her lips

The nectar of celestial Honey

Both join and give birth to

A Fine-looking damsel

Thus she is acclaimed as the progeny of Himalaya

And daughter in law

Of the historical province of Madurai….!

Dancing with tinkling bells on earth,

She builds a tower of melody,

She battled the rogue elephant

As she interweaves the knots folds of celestial music!

In the sound of bangles,

She breaks the rainbow

And intertwines it

Into the unstable fabric of clouds,

As she touches the naval with her hands,

She writes sweetheart tales

And attires this adoration in love costume..!

 At the session of

Embracing shoulder-to-shoulder

The sword assumes a bath

In the river of war…!

The peafowl of long feathers

That pledge jumps on the

Broad chest of the courageous warrior …!

She exposes the shore

As she carries the soul

Upon the eyebrow's enticement

In coral petals

She performs the music

On the Veenai of love

On her youthful floor

Coral jasmine,

She is, Pour the seasoned toddy

Through the pot

As it spills excessively

She harnesses the faded love of quill

And wear it on her shoulder as a sari..!

On a bed of sandalwood

She pours a crush of betel leaves

Thus caressing….

As she ingest the cloves and cardamom

She gluts woozy...!

As the heaven and earth

Touches her love

Her eternal love rises in the sky

And, thus becomes a horizon...!

In the love assemblies of

The blue sky, the moon and the clouds

Her eyes ramble and feel sleepy

In the womb of the celestial fish…!

Here,

The mother of love clans

Summon her to be a daughter-in-law...!

The wives of the king Archunarajan

Observe the flourishing fountain of love

In counting countless sands of river...!

And the 'midnight' melts and falls asleep

At the foot of the 'dawn'…!

As the sky Ganges spills.

The raga of the auspicious scale of morning scatters..!

The dawnless sky is

In the loom of love…!

The eternal scripture lives

In the maiden's bedroom...!

A budding diamond star

Dissolves in the eyelashes

Of the delusion allure beauty…

In that blue sky

It paints the flower face of time god…!

Politeness, gift, cleverness, punishment

These are four weapons of the author

The portrait of strength…

The character of charity…

The Time God…too

All are like crushed scrap papers….!

*****

21. You are the Bharathi

You are not just a piece of paper

Floating in the air

A mature pearl in the sea!

From dawn to our night moon's ray

You are Bharati; our fire of heart!

The Lamp of our home

You are the flame

In our courtyard of sacrifice!

Our heart speaks in your verses!

Oh, Bharathi!

You have stimulated the pain of death

In your departure, only in your demise!

*****

22. The Darkness at Deepavali

The black market hoarder

Lives within the town

The shaggy hair man is reside in a slum

The Tornado blows in our hearts-then

Why do you celebrate the festival of lights?!

Girl:

Wood for burning stove

Selling in a diamond price!

Hot water has not been seen in the near times!

Even the stock of rice and grains has halved!

Male:

During bathing my sweating body was

Was covered in torn striped cloth

Our eyelids filled with worries

Of black smoke…

In our trouble the passing

Festival of lights

Darkens the dawn of our day!

Girl:

The sky is our festival cloth

The weeping child is the fireworks of the festival

Fermented Rice is our festival feast

Beetles and nuts substitute our festival sweets!

Male:

Poverty laid the foundation of the palace!

We trusted the river fish and lost! -and

We left the pond fish too!

Girl:

We consume water and wind

We wobble, however…

We trust in fate

And bend like a bow

Male:

Understand the truth and unite together

The working class must stand up

Let the whole world rejoice in the feast

May the ploughed field should bear the yield!

Girl:

During the Festival of Lights,

We light the lamp

To drive the darkness away -and

Live with light and a smile!

May poverty be wiped out all over the realm

And, let all the people work and live!

*****

23. My Song

I am going to recite songs

In a string of abundance melodies

I position myself as free and

Expressing truthfully from my heart!

Wearing muddy attires

Dining on fermented rice

Proceeding to the field for harvest!

They...

Coming back with empty hands towards

From the opposite side of the river bank

After crossing the water flow!

Paddy grains…

Hits the mound of the harvest field

Falling off like tears of the deprived!

As he works hard on the land

The sternum breaks! –and

Anxiety is born!

Inside the homes of the hard workers

There is a fragrance of

Night flowering Jasmines!

In the grove of areca trees

The entire palm leaves explode!

The star giggles

In the early dawn

Like a fleck of grain!

The waterfall, roaring-and

Chiming with anklet bells!

Like the evening moon

The Sun rises there!

*****

24. The Arch Poet..!

Like the infinite sky

Viewing in tiny eyes

He became the wisdom

That traces my thoughts!

He is a flood for the thirsty sand

He is the Oil that lights the flame

He is a gentle wind that blows the flute!

He rules all the dreams

He is a kingdom of Love

He is an arch of poetry

He is a stream of epics!

The arch poet

His smile glowing brightly

Like the lightening of clouds

He shed tears like a monsoon shower

He flowed like a perennial river of life

He was a bee cherishing

in spirit cup of a spring!

As if the sky twisted into a desert

He passed away!

He painted a poetic work

Of genius landscape!

In the last darkness of the blind eye!

If I were to invite an unknown girl,

I shall call her

As a garden of eternal bliss of love!

If I were to praise the sky

 By another name,

I shall call as "The mother of light"!

If I were to appeal to the earth

By another name

I shall call it" The Inn of Humankind"!

What is innovation?

I shall define using your name,

'A night jasmine' flower

Blooming in old manure!

I shall call poetry by its name

'From an infant to a sighted deity

It was built by verses of classic slang

So that it could be taken by hand....'

I name the Poetry as "Kannadasan"!

*****

25. The Daily News

While reading the Daily Newspaper

Every day impressions like a festival day!

It dissolves the mountain of currency..!

This is working for the underprivileged!

Realise a piece of laughter

Like a small fireworks!

Listen to the street devotees

Of Lord Shiva's songs

And let the politics materialize!

Expressing, the current affairs

Of the country in four lines!

Reading the special edition

On every Sunday,

The readers are soaking in an oil bath

Even the rationalist

Enjoying horoscope columns secretly!

Let the rickshaw absorb the library of the poor

The Rig-Veda convert

These modest cottages into temples!

Adithanar insisted the poor

To read his publications!

This is the footprint

This is the dictionary

Once you read it,

You can understand it line by line!

Headline Shining

Like an elephant's tusk!

In authentication

Betrothals are assured

Through advertisements of matrimonial!

Inspiring the vernacular slang with pride- and

Leaving the green parrots

Flying and joining in the slums!

We are Tamils;

We hail from barracks of passionate Tamils

The sword that fights for justice every day!

A classic drama that makes you laugh

Like Denali Raman!

A mother's shelter,

That balances the

Sentiment of Tamil -

A buffet for the nation too!

Tamil script to be understood

By the eyes of the poor

A newspaper that speaks

Justice on paper – and

Reciting the justice of epic,

Read it and read it

Brother….

And move ahead..!

Become a Tamilian...

Become an Indian...

Become an enhanced global man

A daily newspaper

That raises the heads of Tamils

I have come to sing this…

I am a honey bee!

Pollen spills with celebrations...

Religious elephant explodes...

Daily news that speaks for the festival spirit

Oh dear! Classic people are there, trusting you!

Eradicate the evil of hunger

Rub the poor man's head with oil

You are the bee that drank the poison

We shall host the poor

With the sweetest feast!

The music of social justice vibrates the world

Let the facts be the ruler

May the news editions win!

Long live Tamil Nadu!

*****

26. There is no Space for an Angel

Many nights were blooming...

My memories are following you!

You are a golden moon

Shining smiles in the historical land of King Chola!

In the charming courtyard of Cupid

Hands carrying flower arrows

Thus mesmerized

The sword warrior Vanthiya Thevan!

Kunthavai Theeviyee!

An enchanting soft moon was the praiseful

Clans of Sundara Cholan

The pride attains beauty

The beauty attains pride, too,

You are one who ever born

The combination of

Performing Art and Wisdom,

You moved into the heart

And bloomed with the effect

Of pleasure spring garden!

I dropped you from my fantasy sense

And freed you to stroll around

The Bank of Cauvery!

My dreams vanished!

Your appearance dissolved!

I could see a girl moving

Wearing ancient clothes with plenty of holes

A daughter of King Chola is strolling

Yourself burning in the flame of gloom!

*****

27. Lullaby of a Perennial River…!

We are boatmen of the dark time river

Our eyes are beacon lights...

Our nights never turn into bright

As our skin is in thick tone..!

The values of my race flow

As deep as perennial rivers

And elevate high as the peak of mountains –Still

Our life shelter in the dustbin!

We purify the crowns of the imperialists,

And on the steps of their palace

We fall like soil dust!

Those who delight in our songs at night,

Why don't they hear our cries during the day?

Having constructed pyramids,

We have turned into walking mummies,

This perennial river of dark times flows unceasingly,

Singing lullabies for the anonymous somebody else…!

Those who enjoy our songs at night,

Why don't they hear our cries during the day?

After having built the pyramids

We have become like walking mummies

This perennial river of dark times flows without sleep,

Signing lullabies for the anonymous, somebody else…!

*****

28. The Black Land of Poor

Male

The cotton module occupied is one hundred...!

Tomorrow, the market shall be convened...

Search for a sari and buy fireworks

Let's go together

You may sing a song...!

Girl

With hard-working labour,

we fetch the firewood from the forest

Let's do a party on Diwali

Let's eat sweets and laugh…!

Male

I wear the silk sari –And

I bring variety eatables- Please do come

We all go to grandma that time

I do compose a song for you while you listen

I am sure you will feel sweat and thirsty

Girl

I am tender milky rice

You are the powerful river with force

The person who came to catch the eye is enchanted!

My heart beats to hold your shoulder..!

Male

Leave the paddy field

Don't detach straws from paddy on the harvesting floor...!

Rice from gross does not fulfil the hunger

And my dot, dear it does not sweat on this gold rock

Is it justice to set fire to the gold rock?

I shall come wearing a new sari

Let us laugh and celebrate in the orchid!

*****

29. We the People

On this earth, we bring lanterns in our hands

We experience the ashes,

With tears rolling down our cheeks

Searching for dreams in our hearts!

After putting the quilts warm fit in singing

We live in silence

Flowers blooming in the summer

And thus, we become an oasis!

We came to sow the treasure!

We have found a gold field in the soil

After drinking poison

We have brought out the springs!

At the lame man's feet

We added the hurricane!

We are garlanding pearl oysters

With a string of precious pearls!

Gathering honey under the moonlight,

Pouring it thus in the darkness!

Gazing at the river of the Ganges,

We strain, swimming in the air!

*****

30. At home, in nature

The new spring adorns the flower bed,

The first spring of Indian independence

Respect the tricolour flag.

Nationalism shall not blossom if terrorism is the seed,

If nationalism is the seed, terrorism will be eradicated!

They grow flower plants by uprooting,

Even the wicks of bombs,

They will turn the ashes of the subversive gang

Into a fertilizer for patriotism!

The elders lowered the English flag,

The younger ones hoist the mother's bell flag!

Non-violence pours water

On a fire and dams a flood!

Adaptation from Na.Kamarasan.   In English Sanna Ratnavel

They hoist the flag of widening India

By roping the slave animal itself!

The national flag of our country flies

Above the grapevine

That fertilizes the volcano!

In immemorial time

India had endured slavery,

The Heart Speaks

Today, the heart of the Himalayas speaks!

*****

31. Woodpecker Birds

The human gods,

Woven once…And,

Fell to the ground…!

They laughed with many faces,

At the same time gathered,

Without harm!

The flowers of the faceted mountain,

Sway in the icy wind!

Children run here and there,

Biting tapioca like sugarcane,

At the gate of the village!

Adaptation from Na.Kamarasan.   In English Sanna Ratnavel

You created enmity,\

To divide men!

Man discovered fire to divide the nature!

Woodpeckers, injuring the trees…

Man enjoys listening to that sound,

As a melodious song...!

You created enmity,\

To divide men!

Man discovered fire to divide nature!

Woodpeckers, injuring the trees…

Man enjoys listening to that sound,

As a melodious song…!

*****

32. The 'U' Turn of River Sindhu

A cold wind blows there,

The "Mosquito song" shall be heard.

In the early morning snow,

A person's voice waves!

The old woman organizes

Empty gunny bags,

Precisely keeping them in order...

And she built the tent,

As she chews the betel and nuts,

She looks at the tent!

A shapeless old-age quilt

She melts...

She wanders in search of her rights...

Within the conjuring of relationships!

She sings the soul of music,

Next to the Hindu temple,

In the tent of Islam..!

An old woman named 'Aisha',

She speaks half a word.

She suffers from the cruelty of

Whooping cough,

Yet she does not abhor the temple.

She is a woman at the age of toothless,

But lives of the opinion,

The mosque is the same,

The gate of the heaven is the same!

This is a tent of a widow,

She lost her better half in the religious riots,

And created the tent to live

Near to the Hindu temple!!

On the aggression of the 'Sindhu River' bank,

An imprisoned piece of land

Attained independence!- and

Since then it has confronted mass violence!

A victim girl, A beautiful girl named Aisha,

A warrior called Khan Muhammad,

Engaged the young woman as his spouse!

Snow freezes in the Himalayas

And touches the sky,

Like a reservoir of seed.

In the flood of enmity's sudden war,

The idea of a warrior forced to

Enter the battle, as fire-

And returns in the form of smoke as he is killed!

Below the crescent flag,

Aisha turns like a half-moon,

And cried with countless sorrow!

What if anyone is alive...

What if someone dies?

On the journey of life,

As the banyan tree grows

Death comes every day!

If the beginning ends,

Everything is just the beginning!

Somewhere

When the tomb is built…

Elsewhere,

The cradle is also rocked!

This is life - destruction and creation,

Don't go around and around,

It plays dual roles in our lives!

Life is like a 'drama' theatre!

Aisha walked…

For a thousand days…

Through the mountains!

She crosses the mountain,

She crosses the river,

She drenches when it rains,

She desiccates in the sun,

She continues her journey,

Looking for the banks of Cauvery!

In the province of Yamuna River,

Prolonged violence and riots!

Like the Negro and the white man

Confronting Hindu-Muslim brothers!

In the flowing homeland,

Of the scripture of life,

She leaves the study area,

Of death penalty,

In search of humanity,

Aisha endures her voyage!

Adaptation from Na.Kamarasan.   In English Sanna Ratnavel

In the capital city of the extreme south of India,

On the side of a slum street,

At the walking path of Hindu goddess..!

She pitches the tent,

And reciting the Quran!

There is the Tabernacle of Jesus,

A church on the opposite side!

The verses of female saints of lord Krishna,

Flow gently along the tender wind..!

She harnesses all religions with one blanket,

Leaving the conflicts of regions in the air!

This is a celestial land!

A tea shop,

A street with mutton stalls,

Also a birthday cake shop,

All on one street…!

Designates conflicts of religions on Death Day!

That is also a man's birthday!

Death chases her, throwing a net,

An adventurous, old lady with a tent,

She sells flowers, and…

She buys a new pot and cooks...

Even if the countries split,

Hearts do not separate,

The breeze blows through the forests,

No obstacle to the wind!

Veiled Aisha lives on the corner,

Of the street with…

Three religions' place of worship,

As if drinking the elixir of life in the wind!

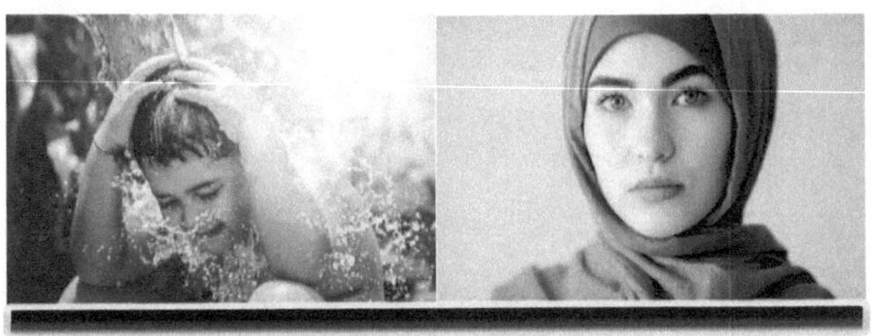

She has no son or daughter,

But she became a mother,

Bathing slum children,

Like little quilts,

With singing a song!

There is the sound of the waves of the Indus River

She asks to come back..!

*****

33. The Divine Lamp

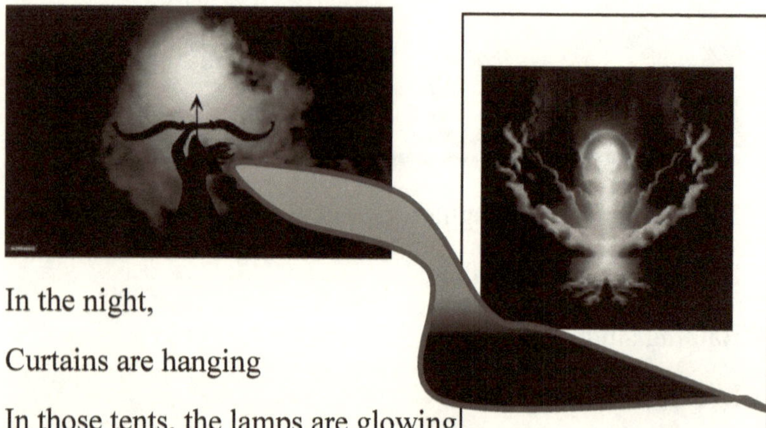

In the night,

Curtains are hanging

In those tents, the lamps are glowing

Grape juice feeds like oil for lamps,

On the lamp, a piece of cloud lightning

Glows like a flame...!

They are not lamps; it is a long smile of justice,

 That habitually burns injustice...!

This is a different kind of Oil bath,

Somehow, the ungodly child...

Has come to the lap of the deity of justice...

Thus she put the heat on the fire thread,

And burns the species of injustice,

Now the injustice has vanished

Along the wind..!

*****

34. APPU (Dear Kamal- Pan Hero)

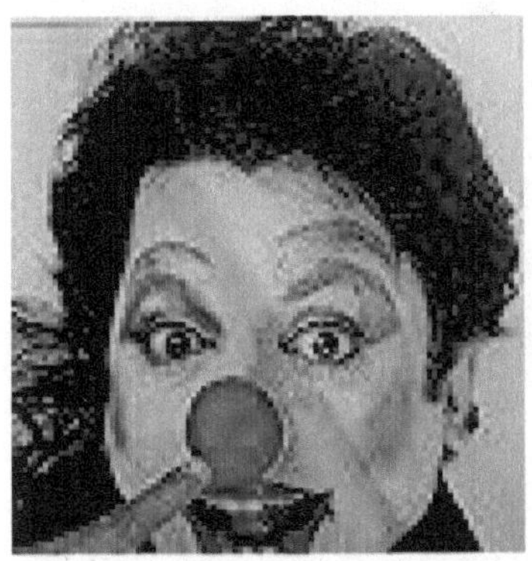

By lessening your tallness,

You have touched the pinnacle of acting!

You have done it through truth,

Never too late to say, it's you!

The 'Eighth Wonder' of the world!

I often think about it…

Many have given it a thought;

No one can exceed the boundaries

Of actor 'SIVAJI' in the world of Acting!

All that happens to make him proud,

Now he is proud of you too,

HE, the crown of actors- thus

You, the crown of ACTING ARTS..!

And have become a fan of

Performing arts too!

In the failure of romance in a circus tent,

You rise to the level of an epic.

Oh! Our sweet "Appu"!

At the Registrar's Office,

When the gold ring was removed

From your finger,

It aches me deeply I place it on the throne of my heart

And celebrate your coronation

By crowning you with a golden crown!

You inaudibly grieve...

When your mother...

Disapproves your appearance!

I was not sad at that time

As you were making

A 'Classic' manifestation on your face…

Because it was in that scene

You are scoring

The eldest son of 'Mother Arts'!

"Appu" is an icon of elephant,

Depicted at the ninth 'Asian Games',

Kamal has the strength of an elephant,

While 'KAMAL' in the costume of the role 'Appu'!

The RAVI VARMA of Novel World 'JANAKIRAMAN'

Rendered that APPU,

Even as not a child of his mother,

In his modern classic novel,

"The sins of APPU's Mother"!

But you have tuned into the Much-loved Child…

Of the 'Mother Celluloid World!

*****

35. The Dreams of Rainbow

That rainbow broadcasting; Our dreams!

All the great poets of the world

In their mother tongue

Tried to express myself but lost,

Your tears of love and sadness,

Conveys me..!!

Is love a consecration of blessing?

Or Is it an invasion of the army?

I still don't understand,

Because it first crowns the heart,

Then lay the pair of handcuffs!

Love comes as the shadow of a shadow in the eyes,

When it falls into the heart,

It turns into the heat of the sun!!

Adaptation from Na.Kamarasan.   In English Sanna Ratnavel

I often have a doubt,

The first people's assembly of democracy

Must have gathered to defeat

The resolution of love!

A flood of light spread like fire on angelic faces,

Falling to ashes in a solar wind,

Declining into the valley is cruel!

In the literature on lovers,

Cupid shoots an arrow,

But in the real world

It is religion and caste,

That shoots arrows at them!

When asked a question

About what's going on here…?

I am unable to answer to my heart!

Like buying fish in the market,

And throwing it in the sea!

In this world market

No saviour has come yet...

And send us back to the sea of love!

The wind blows here

May stop our breath…

Let's leave this shore!

Hurry up….!

*****

36. A Million Crescents

Blooms profusely, spreading its leaf

Writing your name in the

Extract of the red flower...

I sing my glory of gold

I bow my head and salute you with my wishes!

Honey drops spill in all four directions

Of the flower garden

The deer jumps here and there,

And the bees play in a joyful mood

When I sing your praises

With a flower in my hand!

The sky drinks honey in the moon

A silverfish jumps in the sky!

In the falling roots of the banyan tree,

I shall set a beautiful swing

In which I joyfully

Sing the dreams of my heart!

A candlestick….

The lamp is glowing

On the stand by the wall

In the darkness of our time…

The bright light is our gift!

Oh... You are a musk deer?!

Oh, you are a fish of the Cauvery River?!

Oh…you are a street of Chariots!?

Oh…You are the other name of the divine!?

We build a golden fort… …

And a cradle made of flowers…

We protect you without blinking our eyes

You are the Epic!

And a precious

Painting too!

In the surge, the height of a man at the ocean

In which we dive and bring pearls…

And we spread all those pearls

Under your feet

Oh… Sandalwood water

And Rose water sprayed on you,

And the palm civet round dot

In between your eyebrows,

You are a precious gift of Mother!

You have the fragrance of the fiche flower

You have tied the crescent moon

To place a beautiful round dot

In between your brows

The mother of victory shall make her presence!

A bee comes to rejoice

The birthday of the flower

This spring comes on

To cheer the birth of the earth!

The colourful rainbow appears

To wish the birth of a shower

Oh, the classic semantics of Tamil come here

To delight your day...!

*****

37. A Tender Maid

White snow sprinkling the saffron dot,

Marked on the mermaid's forehead,

Leaving the hut with green pots,

Getting on the coo train to trade tender coconuts,

Oh, tender girl..!

Oh..! The eggs of the coconuts,

The lovely shaved doll,

Playing at the elbow of the Virgo,

Oh, tender girl..!

Everyone notices her,

Exclaimed the creator,

Thus she is a festival chariot,

Built with tongue and words,

Oh, tender girl..!

She composes dreams- and

Scores at the vibration of her bracelet,

She is a clan of palm juice,

And thus sweetest tender water,

May she look like an invader?

But it modish dance of the hip,

Oh, tender girl..!

In the back, you carry the sweetest coco tender juice,

Tell me the price of the pearl of tears in your eyes,

I posed at her – She replied,

'The clue is with the salt maker,'

And the pretty rush away with a gloomy face,

Oh, tender girl..!

*****

38. A Play of Love

Espousing you as goddess queen of beauty,

Fusing your reddish lips into sweetness,

As I hold you close,

And thus engaging my tender kiss

On your reddish lips!

Searching for you in a coconut tree grove,

Hence absorbing you in the glad honeymoon,

When time pushes me to leave you,

Screaming sobbing,

I see your face over again,

As the bamboo trees nodding around,

The full moon jerks with milk spray,

You appear in my joyful dream,

Thus you burn me with your gorgeousness!

Observing you as a parrot,

Wandering on the other side of the river,

A small quill invites me to get into the groove,

Agonizing on the striking arrow of EROS,

Besides intently waiting for your footfall,

Embracing you as goddess queen of beauty…!

*****

39. The Stranger

As my mother carries me,

I assumed writing poems,

She gives me birth,

And milks me with her lullaby!

I begin to recite after merely knowing three scales,

My breath swing carries my poems,

As I learn to walk!

I have never changed the colour,

It has never been nested and nested,

I never climbed the tower,

By selling my rules!

Hence no one to get along with and hold my flag,

I don't even own a house to live in...!

The boat that went to the other side did not

Reached the shore!

As my drama within the closed curtain,

The council did not meet even once…!

Far and far I walked,

And never touch the sky!

Adaptation from Na.Kamarasan.   In English Sanna Ratnavel

There is no line for me

In the tiger and goat game,

I am a painter enhancing colours

To spring flowers too!

I have already walked out

From the slavery life

Yes, I am a Wayfarer...!

*****

40. My Cot Room

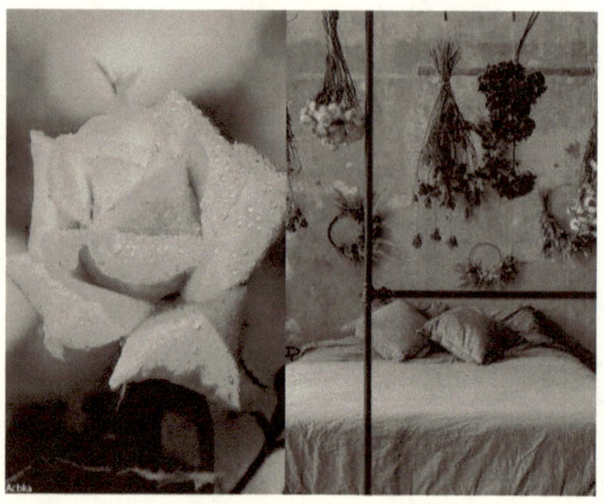

I am a distant kin and kith,

Unable to touch you,

And sleep on the beach,

After the inhabitants, all went to rest

A while later, I woke up and started my creation,

As I don't adore the affection,

I stand near the tent of tears…!

Again over again, I ooze,

And wander like a sceptical man,

Looking for her shoulder

In the temper of throbbing and frenzying!

In the iron workshop,

I keep the strings of drenched flowers,

I arrange to grab it,

And spread at her feet!

After losing the flowers,

I was searching for someone,

And singing like an orphan…

I lost the place of my gratitude,

And unable to restore my bonding,

I disengage the link too…!

I lost my cosmic eyes,

On the soil, I stand blind,

I kneel as I adjust to being physically challenged,

I walked to the milky moon!

I walked in the desert on a bright sunny day!

I came to narrate a drama,

But asking for riddles!

I came here to recite a poem,

But beaten up by musical instruments!

Still, do not realize the time for my rest

In an eight-foot trench!

Myself ascertaining my cemetery,

As I lean on my cot!

*****

41. The Village Angel

Tell a story with both eyes...

The majestic deer standing there.

She poses with both hands,

Looking like

Garlands of flowers around her neck…!

Do you recognize the sign?

Tell me who she is...!

She milks the blood,

Turning the night into a day!

By harnessing with kisses and gentle swaying,

Bathing them in the courtyard…

Thus, she brings up her children,

The golden lamp of the female clan...!

She is the flower of the spring,

Like the grain of the field,

And three kinds of popular fruits

Thus she is the fully productive land of mankind..?

The wind of the Banyan tree,

The song of waterfalls...

Mesmerized as she listens,

Oh! She is the village goddess..?

If the god of Brahma...

Stops the creation of women,

The world turns into dust,

She articulates the message silently..!

She is the shadow of time,

She is the meaning of the epic,

She is a mother within the earth,

And see, there is the goddess of food…!

Women are eyes of the life,

Women are beautiful goddesses,

They live and protect the earth,

Tell them all the time,

All we stand with folding hands..!

*****

42. This is not a Begining..!

In this age…

The bright moon rules the night…

But man claims ruler of the moon,

Hence the science has turned

A 'Vedic' syndrome,

The Vedic mythology was

Thrown away and scattered,

As mere mental fortresses in old bookshops...

The sweetness of hard work

Turns a spectator of bloodshed violence,

The roses are planted

In the wounds of the blood,

Caused by the thrones!

In the Golden Temple,

The mining camp of

Hitler was created,

In the place of god,

There is no beginning by the creators,

Because the creation itself is the "Beginning"

I am a shadow,

My epic is Shadow of Shadow,

But it is not Darkness…!

It is a hidden new flood,

That is the third world..!

*****

43.Hello Hamlet..!

Like going to dive

In a salt pan for gathering pearls,

The songs of independence shall

Echo in this slum..!

Like setting fire to the seed paddy,

The sunlight burned those poor people!

In the slimed eye-opening,

Views of the extensive natural world,

Their scenes are also shrinks!

Even their sky has fallen off

Like a fallen star!

Children of that hunger,

They were warming up next to the sun!

To their crescent moon,

The full moon hasn't come yet!

Like sinking into the depths of darkness,

They were looking for the light!

Like a ruined temple,

Worshipful human culture was changing there...!

*****

44. The Gross Lawn of Villages

The sound of the formless

Coloured the grass field with drifting rain,

Making in a patterned silence!

A small riot occurred in the

A peaceful corner of the earth in the

Northeast,

It resembles the sound of scattered coconut!

Without swimming or sinking or shoring

A tender swimmer stood firm,

Without dreaming- and

Without observing renunciation-and

Without sinking into the shadow of crying

A childhood that nurtures life as a pastime!

Adaptation from Na.Kamarasan.   In English Sanna Ratnavel

As larks herding the sheep

The women begin to sing!

In a semi-deficient grazing ground,

A goat, which looks happy,

It sounds like lord Ganesha...

Thus scored victory in a task...

By circling the mother and father…!

The teeth smile laugh

While grinning over and over again

The earthen root tuber -and

The fruit of the tree!

When the legs are in an open field

Hands proceed like opening a dam!

All through the seasonal rain...

The kings of this country

They painted portraits in the soil!

In an open meadow

Inside the pool of the village

The summer wind was playing around...!

*****

45. The Sky Bird

Appearing like heavenly flowers

The plane landed on the ground!

The ocean of people

Rising above the voice

Of the waves in the walk!

As if the temple

It self-had become a sacrificial platform,

Hearts, which discharge poisonous gas

Aiming to eradicate fashionable attire!

As a bird returning to its nest!

A rationalist comrade returns home

After touching the sky

Of reasoning during travels abroad!

Like the maidservant owning a camel,

A thought longing in his mind!

Where to relinquish these new habits?!

An aeroplane resembling a small bird

The sky is like a vast tent,

The moon appears like a table lamp…

In the age of science, the world has shrunk

And so the heart also has shrunk!

Silver and gold in the treasury

The food vessel in the hand,

Then, how does a scientific circle

Become a poisonous trophy?!

*****

46. For whom she adorns the flower?

Bury the ivory temple in the darkroom

Climbing the tower in the sweltering heat,

The suffocating fellow belongs to the past times,

Like the smell of dirt, reminiscent of red clay,

In the Monsoon by the river!

Throwing human corpses

In the sea of pearl diving

Lowering the height of the mast vessel

Thus a lighthouse that scatters with!

To the old woman,

Selling spinach

In the street corner,

Desiring of setting foot on the moon!

Opening the door for justice,

To enter the courtyard-but

The councils let it go after it,

Through the back door!

A mind that clings to something,

Clinging to everyone,

And making individuals alone to win

This is a slave society!

The smell of flowers reaches the heavens,

The eagles fly up the root of the rose plant-And

Catch the thorn unaware

For whom did she adorn the flower?!

*****

47. The Towel and Dress

Baby in a bamboo basket

Flute in old man's hand

Child marriage for 'Kannan'...

'Radha' comes next in line!

A blind man is lighting the lamp,

A disabled is in the recliner,

A dumb man is searching for a doorbell

Near the ears of the deaf

There is a temple bell!

Adaptation from Na.Kamarasan.   In English Sanna Ratnavel

An agreement amid contradictions,

Within the jail cell

Advertisements pronounce,

About the arrival of the celestial chariot!

Colourful lace dreams fill the void of rags,

A firewood oven unseen,

The cooking has not been done for many days

Under a thatched roof

Without a door!

Gentle rain

That does not disturb the fog!

No guard,

No belligerence!

Comrade has fallen to pieces,

On the shoulder

Of the 'rational village'!

Comrade wrapped the orthodox customs

Around like a garment!

*****

48. A Dream on Lease

Grief and self-pity

Seek solace within,

The burdened mind

Breaks into pieces!

Remains of a bird in the tower

A Gold coin lying in dust!

Seafarers catch fish in the lake,

Baits lifting the ship- then

Throwing it on the shore!

Insects gain strength on their backs,

A thousand trenches

Awaiting for an elephant!

A wound is on the hands of the dragonfly…

A gold ring adorns the hand

Of a deceitful rogue!

Buying it, because the price is low,

Selling when the price rises,

In the hands of those skilled in economics!

Laughter that conceals tears

Tears hiding behind laughter

The elusive face that comes and goes!

With hands tied at the back

And resting crossed over the legs

Finger-snapping becomes a sloth of leisure…

In the blink of an eyes

The hand touches the sky

And reaches back to its origin!

In a dreamlike existence,

The dead are living..!

*****

49. Goat and Tiger Game

Comrade rationality-and

Comrade old conservative customs

Engage in a verbal conflict,

Like a bipolar battle,

In the village booth..!

Engaging enchanting

The controversies

In the line of processions!

Body temperature rises,

As they enjoy

The pleasant hours of argumentation,

Explaining the debates as they unfold!

The thoughts of comrade reasoning

Showering like monsoon...

Over the flame of sacrifice!

His traditional thoughts

Portraying like…

A calf standing on the sacrifice altar!

It resembles a journey through time!

A constant effort to overcome obstacles

and perpetuate drama!

The gold ring fingers sting –and

Narrating the slave women

To wash the vessels in tears!

Fleeing from the nest to the darkness,

Be the messenger

In the enlightening scientific age,

Comrade rationality

Build a stage verandah in the sky,

The game of goat and tiger game rattles!

The comrade's conservative antiquity,

Jumps into ambiguity

And scratches its head!

*****

50. Confluence of Three Rivers

She is the fostering mother who feeds

The moon on the earth

Looking at the stream in the sky,

Religious life of

Wearing bracelets and hanging rope

Around the neck!

Looking at the stream in the sky

The moon is the mother who feeds on earth

The religious life of wearing bracelets

And hanging rope around the neck!

Looking like a ferry in the sky

The mother feeds

The moon's food on the earth...

The religious life of

Wearing bangles-And

Hanging rope around the neck!

The voice of conscious stages walkout,

As the heartbreaks,

A group of hippies

Hoisting smoke flags on the beach!

It destroys itself

Unable to fight

A Self-Altar Battleground!

The pure blood clots

In the red eye - but

The spot is filthy!

It is the capital

Of comrade despair!

Under the sea

An oyster pearl- and

Rock coral performs

Penance in wetness

The tide flows- and

Wanders- and

Ashore…..

The sea fish seeking

A death in sun rays!

At the spot intersection

Of three rivers

The old mountain river and

The new perennial rivers join,

And they sing a joyful song!

Many other tributaries

Unclear about their future in darkness,

And making their province slang

As screaming tone!

*****

51. A Place for Absconding..!

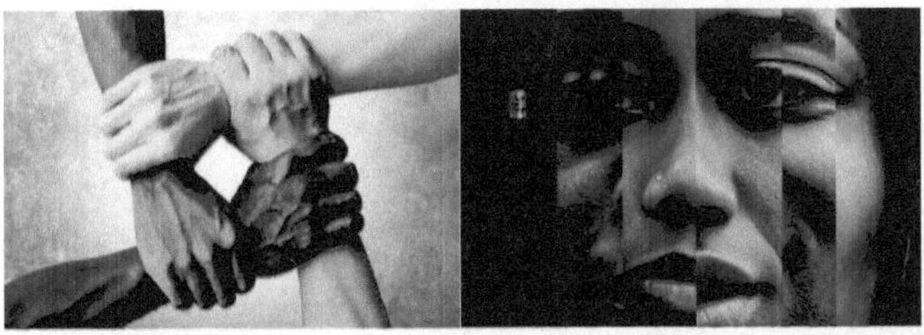

They are the blades of grass of

A superpower nation!

In their motherland,

With one foot trampling the Negro,

And, with the other leg

Touches the moon,

A capitalist paradox!

They talk about the Red Sea

By reading the Bible,

In Vietnam,

The weapons roads of the world war

Jogged through an ocean of blood!

Throwing humanity in the dustbin-And

Building the scientific house...

Those so-called intellectual beings

With the colour of crookedness!

Like a storm that destroys

The lamp of equality...

The darkness jumping

And playing in the lap…

That is the hiding region of antiquity...!

*****

52. The Poisonous Jars

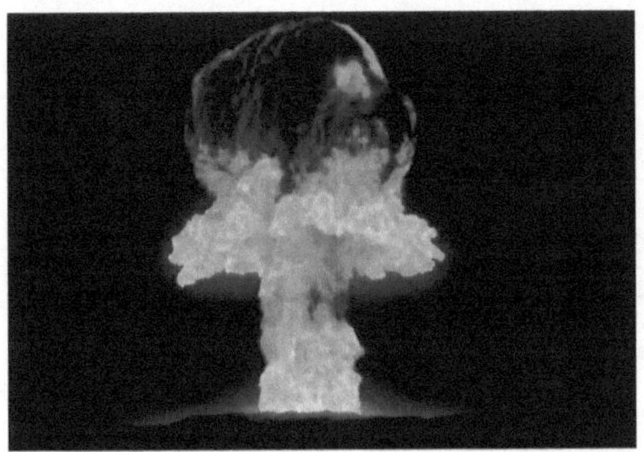

Making the breath akin to the music of clarinet,

And sweating from the weight of the sigh –and

Sustaining a wound on the tongue

Thus they got boiled!

Writing with rays

At the horizon-and

A full golden moon

Shinning in the west!

Assuming the shepherds of the dark people

The Skywatchers,

The mind turns dead and buried in words...

Those cradled in death!

Peace treaties are torn up,

The heart is exposed,

And screaming and hitting the hands!

Signing the agreement

Of nuclear weapons in blood,

Messengers of violence!

Cups of wine fell into the poisonous jar!

*****

53. In the Hands of Devil

The sad telegram of

Lightning striking the cloud!

The rain tears organizing the Garland!

The raindrops are falling,

On the surface of the blue ocean!

A person proceeding to the sea for diving

To make the rhythm of the tide

As a rhythm of his life! –but

He stands with an empty oyster in his hands!

Beauty's dream hole becomes

The key to obscenity!-and

It turns into a brush…- and

Paints the nudes on all the walls!

On top of the church's sweet bread

There are sour grapes!

God standing like a dried tree

This leads to the mental fadeaway of the priests!

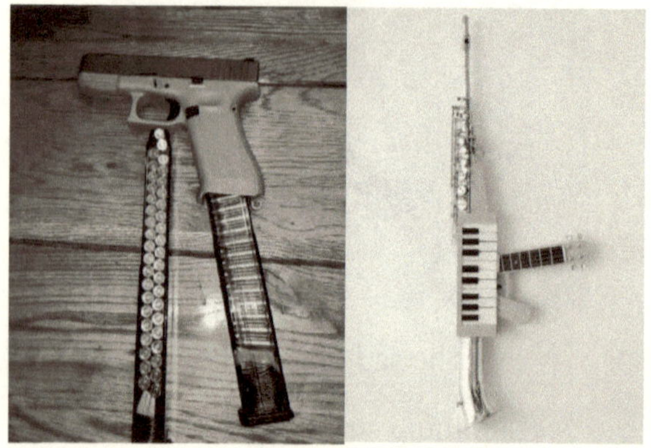

By grace, the devil enters heaven

Finally, the heaven is

In the hands of Satan!

Here the peace talks are progressing

On keeping the guns in the hands!

This is the 'THIRD WORLD'!

*****

54. The PONGAL FESTIVAL

And The Perennial River

The Flagellum blooms above the roof

The paddy fields shall be

Blessed with the pleasant rains!

'Mullai' River is a propensity

And a steady stream of water

Flowing in the west of the town

It sings a song!

The blinking stars

Sprouting in deep darkness

In the classic expressions

Of the harvesting sickle,

Crafting the rhythm of swaying bangles!

A poor mind finds solace

In getting grain malt ketchup

With plenty of men

Gathering paddy rice

In the reaping time,

That celebrates the festival of harvest!

The colourful sugarcane shall be

The new chariot of the festival!

On the moonlit nights

On the banks of this river

Many sighs drive along the gentle wind!

Those who became slaves

In tiling and the field,

Sadness creeps over the shoulder and eyes!

Adaptation from Na.Kamarasan.   In English Sanna Ratnavel

Roots are scapegoats-and

Falling off due to the sun!

You may slip into the oasis

To listen to your cuckoo's lullaby!

I am topless, approaching to sing,

A slender lifelike painting - but

The river waves are screaming!

As the perennial river flows with speed,

All directions 'You Turn" is the fields,

The head of the Banana and Sugarcane shall be

Rose by the spring water!

The tall reddish sugarcane

Looks as tall as a man…

If you eat it, the honey will scatter!

Tears in the eyes of the one

Who came to drink honey?

The human mind dries up

On the banks of the eternal river!

The harvesting festival

Do not harness the poor...!

If the day, of the new festival

Makes the labourers feel glad,

The earth shall be blessed!

*****

55. My Leader…!

In the gloomy darkness

The light of the dawn emerges

As a thousand shining lamps,

Welcome to the historic drama!

At the doorstep of the time

In the deep blackish midnight

We once believed,

That all direction of life was closed!

Still, I say,

The spring itself harnessed the dawn.

Men had lost,

As if the earth had disappeared!

Now

A new heaven has graced there!

Raising the lifeless body,

Breathing life into us,

Awakening our consciousness,

Praising the truth,

I know the story of history,

The world knows the reason!

In the pleasure garden

Flowers bloom on all sides!

Honey scatters in all eight directions

The young wind sings joyfully along!

All the monkeys came to pluck the flowers,

And, those ran away,

Adaptation from Na.Kamarasan.   In English Sanna Ratnavel

The leader of the new era,

Your song reminds like

Cuckoo of flowers garden!

Welcome, our spring breeze!

Welcome to the new era of mankind,

That has come to lay a path

From the earth to above the sky!

Until a full moon day reaches

In the deep blue sky,

The number of star flowers

Giggles at the midnight work!

Wherever the river of life flows

Your voice shall be heard, everywhere!

Filling the social gap,

The poor with bowed heads

Power stands up nearer to the rain shower!

You are an eye-opening epic,

Tenders the justice

Where everyone has everything

We welcome the new flower of time!

As the sky showers water

All rivers flow with honey

The earth is full of flowers

A new age opens the dawn.

Oh! There is my frontrunner

One in thousand

Get used to walking in his way,

The flower blooms alongside him,

Mature as a treasure

Six crore classic peoples

I am the son who dances like a dream!

Oh! There is my frontrunner!

*****

56. I am also a Capital City …!

My name is a synonym

Of the 'Harvesting Festival'!

I am the Capital of Sugarcane!

The National Income of

Livestock! Every year,

The pots of the PONGAL festival are boiled

And offer respectful prayers to the field!

I shall forever remember

Historical classical's bravery

In the bull-harnessing game!

Marriages are not arranged

In the scenes of our anthology verses!

I am a radio

In the province of my youth,

The sound of women's bangles

Mesmerizes the viewers' choices!

More precious than the stars

In the sky,

In my eyes,

The grains of the earth bear colossal value!

My name reflects in the beats of classic dance!

I am a passionate fan

In wedding magazines,

I'll prove to you my skills in palm lines!

I am an enthusiastic follower of wedding invitations;

I shall portray my palmistry skills!

All three of my days are flavoured with

Three forms of the classical language!

Mothers-in-law; who treat daughters-in-law

As divine cows,

I shall influence them to revere

The abundance of cow farms!

The ground appears brown to me,

The plough shaft is my writing tool,

And the rain shower becomes my ink!

In my belief,

A heroic salute offered to the sun deity

From the hearths of fire!

I make the sun shine in

The clothes of the poor man,

Courage and love are the twins that

I gave birth to me

But I am not a mother, but

The cradle of classic Tamizh values!

*****

57. The Rest of Poor Men's Heart

Don't pluck the flowers!

Let them fall and spread the earth!

Don't disturb the Quilt in the orchid!

Let it sing the glory of the hero!

Don't block the wind!

Let's go towards the grave!

Don't stop the tears,

Let the eyes drink seawater!

Every Day is a 'mourning' day for…

The classic language!

The god who granted the boon with

Human nature,

A holy penance,

That witnessed the joy of death!

A heart that was the treasure

Of a poor household

Sleeping here!

*****

58. The Next Page

We are valley dwellers!

Concerning the missing child

As if the advertisement had disappeared

Our life dreams are taken away

And lost now, as well!

We are trapped in the hands of the rich,

The owners of the sugarcane field

In the time of the 'Harvesting Festival'...

We claim wages as usual,

But we end up borrowing

Sugarcane for tasting it, too,

We, the wage workers!

We do sun salutations for not

On account of this festival

But for living in darkness!

What else, we can do?

We, the poor people have no sun

Even as' Eskimos' deserve!

Like a fight, for water on the street tube

The River water disputes

In the countries debate market!

The masters passionately admire their fields!

The wage workers stand there with tied hands!

Masters are the owners of the brush,

In this land!

All paint artists are daily wagers!

The festival's new clothes scratch our hearts,

As seen in today's newspapers!

The yellow water of this festival

It is nothing, but a flow of our tears,

Even my heart thinks like this!

If the Himalayas dry up,

Only the life of

Five perennial rivers shall perish,

But thousands of huts shall be

Replaced there!

One side of the world was always dark

When shall we know the other side?

Once, there was a plain delta,

A New Leader! A New Earth!

People were breathing with hope!

The nation in the street came to the field!

The juice of sugarcane looks like tears!

For those who enter the Dark Ages!

Make it a golden age, too!

The wind was singing when it strolled

The field of sugarcane nods that!

*****

59. The Song of Lullaby

Oh! Flower of the Cradle

Fruits of my napping cot!

Silk of the forest,

Strings of aromatic rose water!

Your eyes are temple bells,

You are a charming maiden

Classic language!

You are a beautiful little crescent,

You are a magnificent yellow peacock!

You are council

Of three versions

Of classic language!

Your face already

Touched the full moon!

You are a Lily flower,

You invited whom here?

I shall play the song

All your night!

The darkest of dark cloud

Knows you!

The drops in your tears

Knows me!

If the child laughs, it is silver

Falling into the ground!

Adaptation from Na.Kamarasan.   In English Sanna Ratnavel

If the River Ganges cries

There shall be a flood in the Ganges!

If you give a kiss

The breeze shall blow me!

If you hug me

The eyes shall read the rhythm!

 In spoken slang

The classic 'TAMIZH' warm the heart!

It cultivates your soul,

And sow the love!

 Oh, my pet storm!

Your twinkle eyes are a flame!

On the silver screen,

The small screen that came!

If lightning strikes

The sky will love you!

If stars sprouts in the sky

Your eyes open gently!

All four directions build

Cradling for your beauty

Poet shall compose songs

For you in all seven notes!

Your silent eyes

That writes magic poetry!

You are a bird that falls

On our chest- and

Swings on our shoulder!

At the corner

Of grass field

Your brightness

Swim in the breeze!

Your voice

That enchants people!

Separated from the mother,

The treasure jumps into the soil!

The mother milk of the tides

Those quench your thirst!

In the ocean that flows

Full of small boats

In the night

The rolling waves

Sing your glory!

The mother is nature,

The home of the father in nature

You deserve to share their love forever!

*****

60. The Divine Rule
Shall Come Back

Oh, Goddess of our heart!

As Judas betrayed and kissed Jesus

Death has overtaken you with silence!

Even when the rainbow shawl

Wrapping around you as an honour

You are the one who loved

Shadows of the slum!

That is why,

The hearts of underprivileged

Even death has no power

To take you away!

When the divine messenger

Put into crucification

His disciples shared his clothes!

We only secured your holiness and

We took it for granted!

A lightning flag

Jesus rose from the grave

Dressed in frozen snow

Your palm of hands turned red

As you gave away more!

You are the showers of clouds,

Cold moon

You have resurrected as wind,

Breath of the heart

And united in our lives!

When a tragic drama postponed

So many times

It's finally over?!

My heart came out,

And hit your grave

And crying over again and again!

Every day

We were releaved from sleep

And go into a long sleep!

Death is an event, too

But it has happened to a HISTORY?!

Like a distant song

From the shore

Still, we hear your sweet voice

It touches our ears!

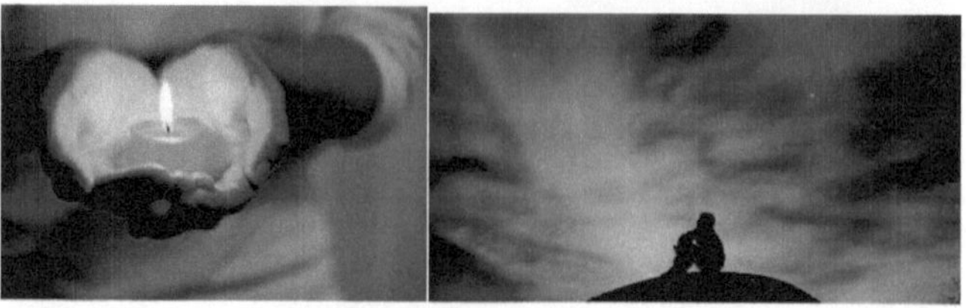

The candles of your temple

Now glowing brightly!

We also cultivate dreams of hope!

Here comes the kingdom

Of our holy deity again!

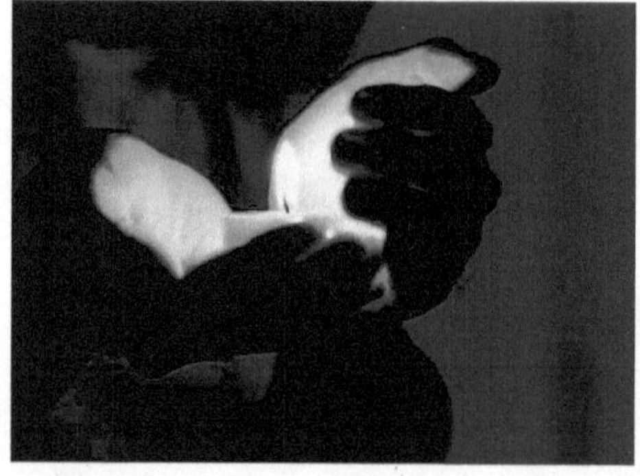

*****

61. My Love and River Tide!

And yet, I bid farewell to you,

My emotions greet the gentle river wave

Again and again!

Oh! Lovely tide of the gentle river,

Come and see the day of her flowering!

Oh! My dear! Agile River Wave,

I welcome you

To bring water to the poor earth!

Now your face is masked

Like the honeyed fruit sleeping in the garden!

I intend to perceive you on the occasion

During the cold windblowing season!

It is time for the moon-like canoe

Reaching the banks of the river!

Be relaxed on your rainy cloud hair

It stumbled that this was more than enough!

During our love scenario,

We enjoyed in the same way equally - and

Looking for pleasure from instant to moment

And the joy of being alive is countless!

The tide quietly breaks into the shower

When I touch the soft river foam flower - and

My head always pretends

To rest at the surface of gorgeous tides!

You profoundly conquer the spring season,

And I sense your joyful occasion

While you are nearing my accommodation!

Blissful colours reside in the vein of rain,

Painting the heavenly pretty rainbow

At the horizon of the sky elbow - and

Gently, you concealed me like the soft petals

By the river of your massive love cordaitales!

At the instant after leaving the wedding stage,

Seeing the spouse is a joyful new evening - and

Your presence as a classic young virtuous girl

Bring welfare melodies of our life song!

Oh, my dear gentle river wave,

I welcome you always with my sweetheart!

Since you bring water to the poor earth - and

I greet you on the eve of her blooming day!

62. Oh Thousand Dreams…!

Oh dreams! Oh, our sweet dreams!

Oh, our thousand dreams!

Oh, the angels of love messengers

Let my caring love pay its visit!

Get my groom some time with me!

You are the painting created using a nail

Her shyness rhymes with painting brush colours

Her face is the substitute for the capital city

And her hands become closed doors of the castle!

Let the lips bloom like the flower

Let the beetles of the heart fly there

Let the ornated handcuffs with bangles crumble there

Let the wings of love rise as high there!

Let the lamp like the moon shine in gleam

Let the deep-sleep nights glow in lustre

Let rhyme poems breed in adoration of love

Let an epic love crawl in the caring cradle base!

*****

63. A Night Singer's Lullaby

A night singer came

He brought two songs to his heart

To the angels that she will wait

He sent one in the breeze

Buddha's face appears

His philosophical flame glimmering

Pictorial eye shining

There are many stories in it!

Ariraro! Ariraro!

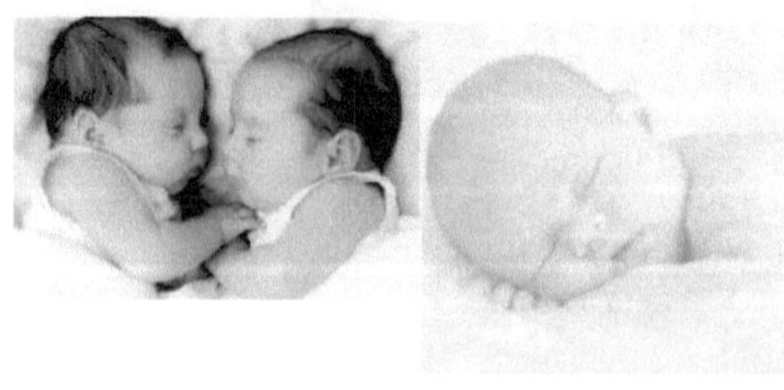

*****

64. Oh My dear deer! And honey!

Oh! doe and hind it is you, my tender girl,

I hoarded you in my range of eyesight

I choked myself in the desire of heart

Rested in addiction, I am none but myself

As the dew at dawn dabbled in my eyes

At that juncture, a lovely dream bloomed in my soul

And your graceful lotus vision looking for me

Hence, the spring season is in full swing!

Thirsty desire engaged in the stage of drama

My thousand songs search for the splendid grandgirl

You are the temple chariot of supernatural being

You are the flower blessed by your angels

You are the milk-soaked honey of the breeze

Blue flower magic shining memories are the sweet

Paintings carried in the love tower crawling in hands

Love god recited mantra to Morphine, the dancing girl

My desire is the king of my heart

The colourful roses that dance in my eyes

You are the glow of my love temple

Oh! My darling, come and shelter in my heart!

*****

65. Honey Moon on the Horizon

Man:
Honeymoon on the horizon
Dances and sings
Let us join there as skylark!
The clouds look like swing bed
Let us also dance and join there
When the scene ends
I shall be your costume!

Man:
I am also hearing the songs of the sky
And holding the fragrance of flowers
In my hands!

Girl:
Let me try to hang the swing
In the bamboo forest
And use the chariot of Love land
To perform my dance skills!

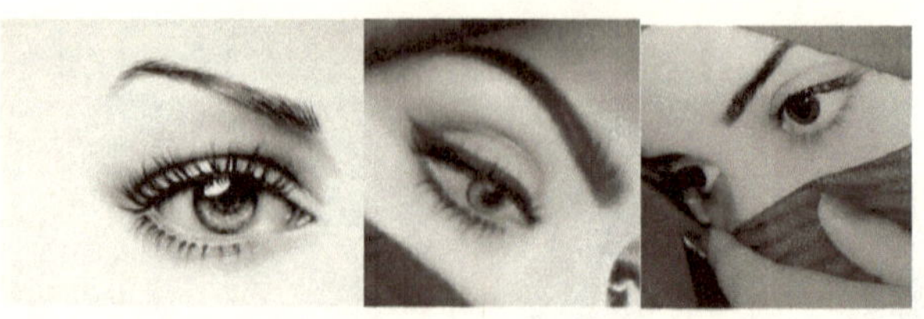

Man:
My love is a splendid flower garden
You are a flower with the skill of expressions
The sky is entertaining us with a lullaby
Hence, let us join in the mood of love!

Girl:
You are the loving flower
Dancing on my chest always
No doubt, I am the one who adorns the flower
As my divine spouse

Man:
You are the eyelashes of a loving king
And embrace him like a creeper on his chest
The divine king adorns you as his angel!

Girl:
Girl: You are an angel flower
Keep garnishing along the human body
Your admirable sight promising
On your stage performance instance!

Man:
You are my divine star
Close half eyes in the moment of our love
You are a sole tune of love god's melody!

Girl:
You are the skin of a king
And I held you out of my love
In the breeze of one fine evening!

Man:
You are a dancing golden cloud
Of the dynamic sky
And privileged as my cosy love temple!

Girl:
Your eyes shining as a glowing lamp
Your fingers in the hands
Sketching thousands of lovely paintings!

* * * * *

66. Love with Forest Prince

The prince of the forest is here

And sings all-day

He asked why there was anger in her eyes

And expressed his love in the classic language!

On the stage of flowers

The prince of the forest sings all day

He blows a tune of love in his flute

On the stage of the flower!

He drops a musical tune from his closing eyes

His flower-like feet sing colourful melodies

He sings all in the gorgeous chariot

Of the Forest prince

And a joyful thirst spills

Out of the sedating toddy pool

All these were born out of love instances!

In the nest of love

The love quilts caressing in affection

The tender girl adorns all colours

In her glittering shoulders

In search of love signs

At the instances, her yellowish cheeks join

In the fine-tuning of the love pitch

And sings classic love lyrics

And looks for its divine relationships

At last, a heavenly love blooms!

The mesmerizing forest prince

Sings from the sky!

The tender girl dances to the song,

Joyful kisses create noises

As the wooden churner of the forest woman,

The evening moon blooms

At the bottom of the horizon

It speaks with a joyous, quiet language

The beetles sing in the honey

Spills from the sunset flowers

The gentle breeze blows with privilege

The forest prince sings

The eyes are closing to hang on the melody

The cheeks in the faces turn into blemish red!

*****

Epilogue

Being granted the extraordinary opportunity to translate the esteemed poet's work fills me with profound gratitude and honor.It's a rare privilege to collaborate closely with a renowned poet and to be entrusted with the delicate task of translating his invaluable creations.

This experience is a humbling reminder of the significance of his creativity, and I approach it with deep respect and a sense of responsibility to faithfully convey his brilliance to a broader audience.

The poet's mastery in intertwining sophisticated word comparisons and vivid imagery in his timeless language is truly enchanting. While his verses often explore the depths of love, they also beautifully depict the wonders of nature, highlighting its profound significance.

Moreover, his advocacy extends beyond mere romanticism, championing a world where gender equality and socioeconomic parity reign supreme.

Sincerely

SANNA RATNAVEL

The Eminent Poet Na. Kamarasan has expressed that his primary motivation for writing poetry and lyrics has never been fame or fortune, but rather a desire to elevate Tamizh literature to a global standard.

Good luck always!

*****